**At a Glance™** Series   DVD and Lesson Book

D0504055

DVD Guitar Soloing

Written by Joe Charupakorn and Chad Johnson
Video Performers: Doug Boduch and Wolf Marshall

ISBN: 978-1-4234-9488-1

HAL•LEONARD®
CORPORATION
7777 W. BLUEMOUND RD. P.O. BOX 13819 MILWAUKEE, WI 53213

Visit Hal Leonard Online at
www.halleonard.com

Table of Contents

INTRODUCTION

Welcome to *DVD Guitar Soloing*, from Hal Leonard's exciting At a Glance series. Not as in-depth and slow moving as traditional method books, the material in *DVD Guitar Soloing* is presented in a snappy and fun manner and will help you learn important soloing strategies in virtually no time at all. Plus, the At a Glance series uses real riffs and licks by real artists to illustrate how the concepts you're learning are used by the masters. For example, in *DVD Guitar Soloing*, you'll learn classic soloing techniques like motific development and repetition in addition to modern, ear-catching scale substitution concepts. This book/DVD covers all the bases for beginning to advanced guitarists. Selections include Lynyrd Skynyrd's "Freebird," Eric Clapton's "Lay Down Sally," Stevie Ray Vaughn's "Texas Flood," and Guns N' Roses' "Sweet Child O' Mine," to name just a few.

Additionally, each book in the At a Glance series comes with a DVD containing video lessons that correspond to the printed material. The DVD that accompanies this book contains four video lessons, each approximately 8 to 10 minutes in length, that correspond to the topics covered in *DVD Guitar Soloing*. In these videos, ace instructors Wolf Marshall and Doug Boduch will show you in great detail everything from universal rhythmic phrasing concepts to the secrets of successfully mixing scale combinations to create unique and exotic sounds. As you work through *DVD Guitar Soloing*, try to play the examples first on your own and then check out the DVD for additional help or to see if you played it correctly. As the saying goes, "A picture is worth a thousand words," so be sure to use this invaluable tool on your quest to becoming a world-class guitar soloist.

ROCK PHRASING

In this lesson, we'll learn some basic methods of phrasing in rock solos. Most solos use multiple phrasing concepts simultaneously or one right after another, but we'll study them one at a time to make them easier to learn.

Rhythmic Control and Repetition

Rhythm is 50% of every melody, so you should keep the foot tapping even when soloing to provide an internal reference for the correct timing of your notes.

The framework of most playing situations is provided by a chord progression, a bass riff, and the drummer. To accurately repeat a phrase, we can learn to play it on the same beat each time. After this skill is established, you can move licks onto different beats for variety.

 Let's practice repetitive two- note groups in eighth notes moving down the E Dorian mode, starting each time on beat 1 of the measure. Be sure to rest for the remainder of the full bar after each group, continuing the verbal count up to 4.

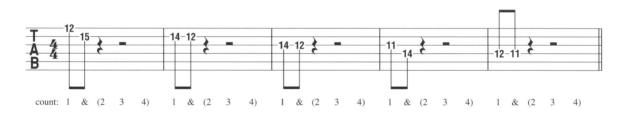

 Now we'll play the same notes but start on the "and" of beat 1 in each measure. Even though we're using the same notes, it "feels" different because it starts in a different place in the measure.

 This time, start on beat 2 in each measure.

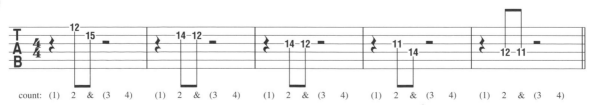

You'll improve your timing and note placement by practicing groups starting on every one of the eighth notes in the measure while counting aloud. Don't forget to ascend the scale also and then try it with longer groups of scale notes.

The solo from Huey Lewis's "Heart and Soul" shows how much mileage one note can get you if you know how to use it. Compare the sound and feel of the on-the-beat versus the off-the-beat placement of the A note.

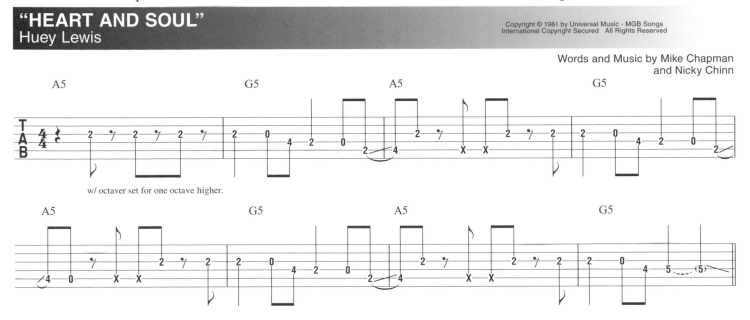

Words and Music by Mike Chapman
and Nicky Chinn

Rhythmic ideas should also be practiced along to a backing rhythm track, so you have a reference point to hear how these rhythmic shifts sound against the rhythm section. The notes will sound and feel different depending on which beat or upbeat they start on.

Defining Form with Space

Chord progressions or rhythm section riffs are usually arranged into phrases of two, four, or eight measures in length. As soloists, we want to define these structures along with the rest of the band, rather than randomly scattering our favorite licks over them. We can do it by leaving some space with either rests or sustained notes.

 To practice defining form while soloing, record or sequence any repeating four-measure progression and loop it for about five minutes. You can buy a looping pedal to record and playback loops or you can use a pre-recorded backing track. The loop doesn't need to be fancy—maybe something like this.

 Now try soloing with only one or two notes in each of the first three measures while still counting aloud. Play a big, fat whole note—usually the root or 5th of the scale—on the downbeat of measure 4 every time it comes around. Measure 4 is a natural finishing place in four-bar phrasing; there's often a drum fill here.

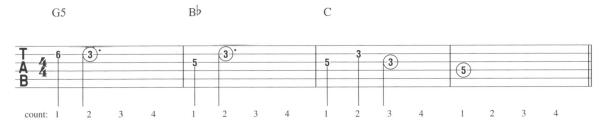

Being mindful of these things will also help you keep your place in a solo.

Motific Development

When a lick is repeated in a solo, new details are often added to allow the listeners to follow your train of thought, because part of what they are hearing is familiar and creates a point of reference for the additional materials.

The possible ways to develop a motif are infinite. For example, you can add articulations like slides or bends to the notes of your original lick. You can use the same pitches but with a different rhythm. You can use the same rhythm but with different pitches, as we'll do in the next example. You can keep the same lick and add one or two notes at the end. All are strong motific development techniques.

In the next example, simple licks are used two or three times each, applying the same rhythm but with different pitches. When a lick is repeated, it's varied by having one or two notes added. To keep things steadily moving forward, those final few notes become the basis for the next lick. This means that the new material is actually the same as part of the previous lick, so it all makes musical sense and has cohesion.

 This process provides a melodic backbone for improvising in rock or any other style.

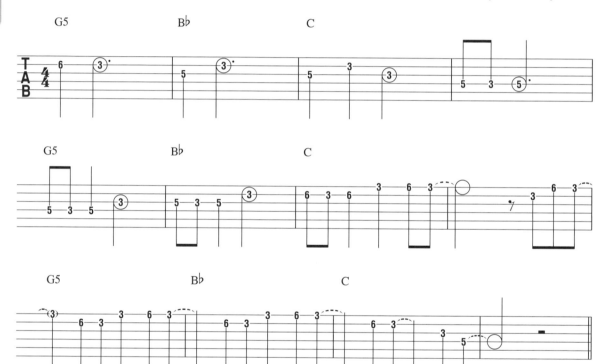

The strong motific development used in the solo of Rod Stewart's "Maggie May" gives it a memorable compositional quality.

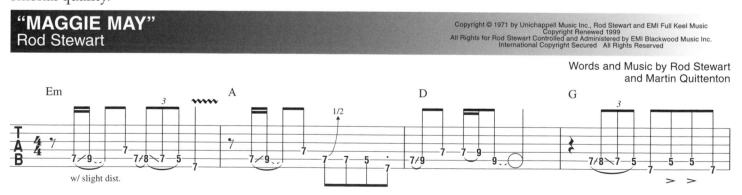

"MAGGIE MAY"
Rod Stewart

Words and Music by Rod Stewart
and Martin Quittenton

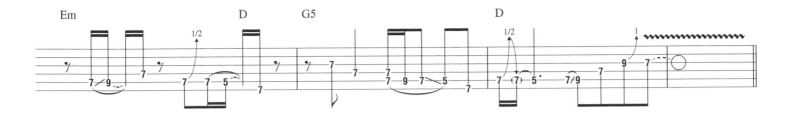

After this structure is established, it's easy to throw in more notes and details like pull-offs, slides, and bends. Your ear can still follow the inherent underlying logic. Watch the demonstration on the DVD to hear this.

Crossing the Bar Line

The phrasing ideas we've covered thus far depend on the ability to count, and especially to keep track of beat 1 of the measure or progression. This can be tricky if you get caught up "in the heat of the moment" and lose focus on where you are, time-wise, in relation to the band.

However, once that ability becomes ingrained and you have a flawless sense of time and meter, you'll be better equipped to pull off more advanced ideas that cross the bar line smoothly and return to the groove seamlessly.

We can divide a 4/4 time signature into smaller groupings of varied rhythms to create more complex riffs and soloing structures. One real classic uses four groups of three eighth notes and two groups of two for a total of two measures of eighth notes in 4/4 time.

Here it is applied to a G minor pentatonic scale pattern. Keep the foot tapping in 4/4 underneath! If you're not used to this type of phrasing, the lick might feel funny at first when you play it against a rhythm section.

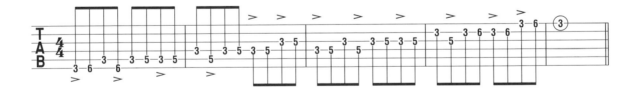

By playing only the first note of each group, you create a cross-rhythm that clearly skips beat number 1 of measures 2 and 4. The notes then last for a beat and a half, which contrasts nicely against the steady 4/4 meter.

In his solo on "Lay Down Sally," Eric Clapton implies this cross-rhythm for several of his melodies.

"LAY DOWN SALLY"
Eric Clapton

Words and Music by Eric Clapton,
Marcy Levy and George Terry

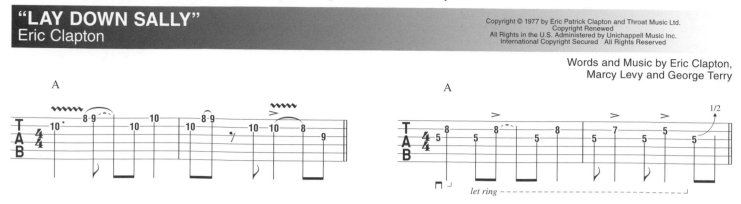

Carlos Santana does the same in "Oye Como Va."

"OYE COMO VA"
Santana

Words and Music by
Tito Puente

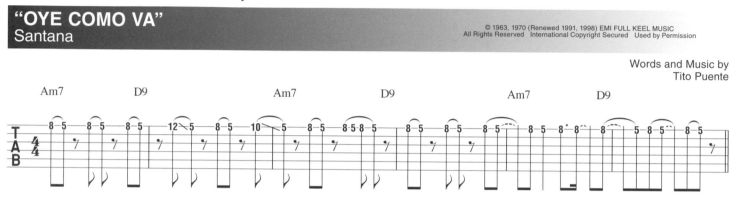

Besides getting the band to play these rhythms in your composition, you can also just superimpose them as soloing devices that temporarily lift you out of the rhythmic structure and drop you back into it.

 Here's a lick from the G blues scale that crosses the bar line using a 3–2–2–2, 3–2–2 structure.

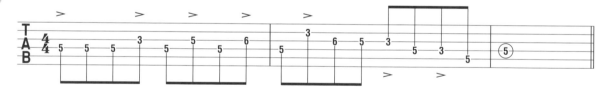

 And here's a G Dorian lick structured by thinking in groups of 5, 5, and 6.

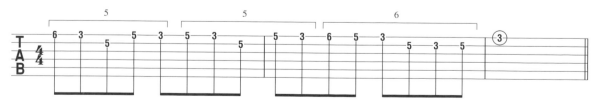

Notice these licks are set up to come out on the downbeat with the tonic of the scale. When you're used to them, you can string together longer sequences to delay that resolution. Just make sure that you clearly and strongly resolve. The definitive resolution is the big "payoff" for all the rhythmic chicanery.

You can also take this idea to the next rhythmic level and do it with sixteenth-based rhythms. Here's an example from Free's "All Right Now" that uses a repeating three-note fragment grouped as sixteenths.

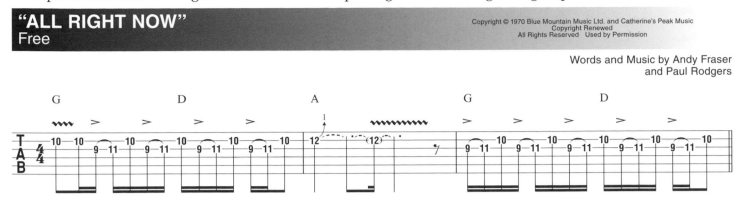

"ALL RIGHT NOW"
Free

Words and Music by Andy Fraser
and Paul Rodgers

And here's a similar idea from The Black Crowes' "Hard to Handle."

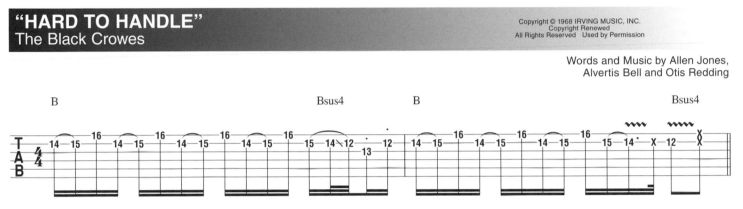

"HARD TO HANDLE"
The Black Crowes

Words and Music by Allen Jones,
Alvertis Bell and Otis Redding

All the ideas we discussed have a strong rhythmic focus. It's vital to stay in the groove and keep track of where the downbeat is if you want a strongly phrased solo.

REPEATING LICKS

If you've spent enough time in your solos playing tasty melodic lines, and you're ready to drive your listeners to a frenzy, you've come to the right place. It's time to harness the power of the repeating lick. We touched briefly on manipulating repeating licks in the previous lesson on motific development; now let's get some of these licks under your fingers.

Pentatonic Classics

Let's start with a few must-know pentatonic licks that no lead guitarist should be without. This first one, in A, is pretty much "repeating licks 101."

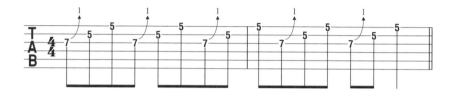

Here's that lick used in Kiss' "Rock and Roll All Nite." This is played an octave higher at the seventeenth fret minor pentatonic shape and has that three-against-four crossing the barline rhythm that we talked about earlier in the Rock Phrasing lesson.

Tune down 1/2 step:
(low to high) Eb–Ab–Db–Gb–Bb–Eb

Words and Music by Paul Stanley
and Gene Simmons

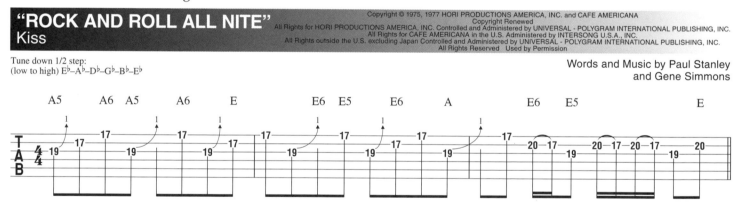

You can pretty much go on and on as long as you'd like…
or you could also speed up to triplets to raise the intensity.

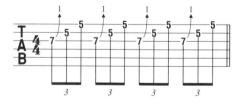

And here's a southern rock one in D that's always ripe for the pickin' in uptempo songs when the band really starts cooking.

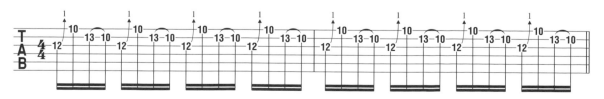

Randy Rhoads took this lick to the next level by blazing through it in sextuplets during his "Mr. Crowley" solo. This one is based on the D minor pentatonic scale.

"MR. CROWLEY"
Ozzy Osbourne

Words and Music by Ozzy Osbourne,
Randy Rhoads and Bob Daisley

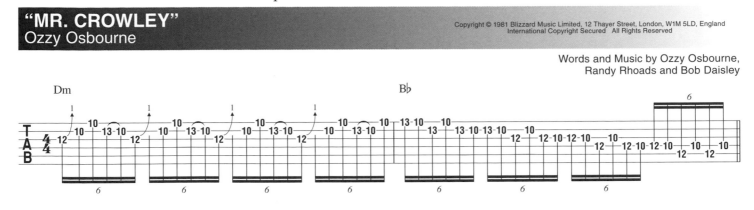

A variation on this one involves moving the lick one sixteenth over within the beat. If you play this one on a mid-tempo tune, you can start in tempo and then keep speeding up until your guitar explodes—or at least until the singer bumps you off center stage.

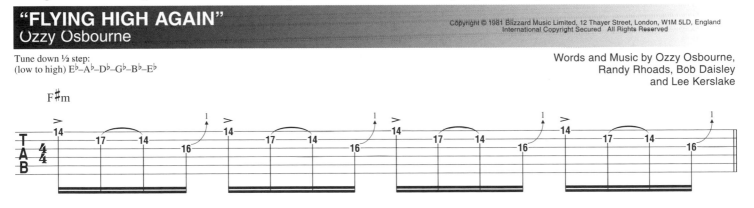

Using the F# minor pentatonic scale, Randy Rhoads does this in "Flying High Again."

"FLYING HIGH AGAIN"
Ozzy Osbourne

Tune down ½ step:
(low to high) Eb–Ab–Db–Gb–Bb–Eb

Words and Music by Ozzy Osbourne,
Randy Rhoads, Bob Daisley
and Lee Kerslake

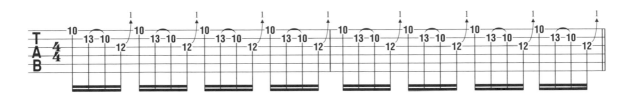

In "Feel Your Love Tonight," Eddie Van Halen creates a variation on this idea by adding in an extra note and also holding the bent note slightly longer than the sixteenths. This one is derived from the C# minor pentatonic scale.

"FEEL YOUR LOVE TONIGHT"
Van Halen

Tune down 1/2 step:
(low to high) Eb–Ab–Db–Gb–Bb–Eb

Words and Music by David Lee Roth,
Edward Van Halen, Alex Van Halen
and Michael Anthony

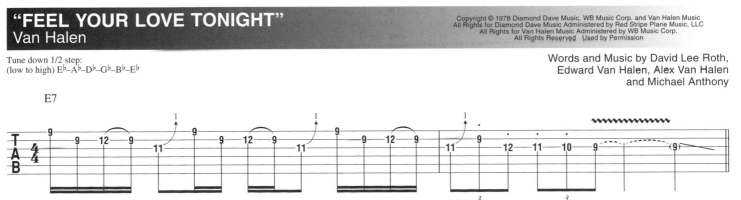

11

Pentatonic shredders Eric Johnson and Zakk Wylde will milk this next type of lick in B minor for all it's worth. You'll need some chops to pull it off.

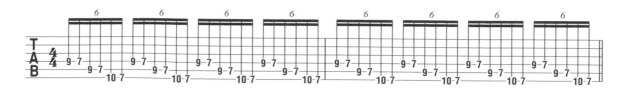

In "Cliffs of Dover," Eric Johnson plays a similar riff based on the E minor pentatonic scale. The trick here is that, instead of an even group of four or six, Eric's using a group of five. That means the picking is a bit more challenging because the downstrokes and upstrokes will flip each time through the lick (assuming you're using alternate picking).

"CLIFFS OF DOVER"
Eric Johnson

By Eric Johnson

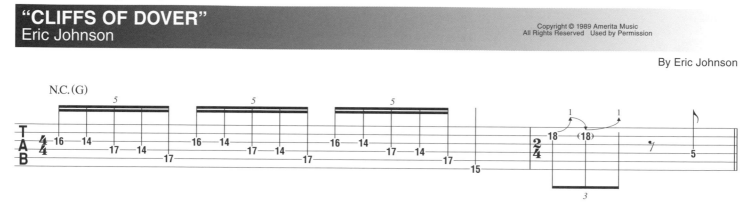

You can move that pattern to any string group in the box shape. Another popular one is here.

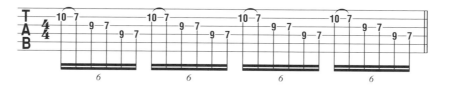

Here's Zakk tearing it up on "Crazy Babies."

"CRAZY BABIES"
Ozzy Osbourne

Tune down 1/2 step:
(low to high) E♭–A♭–D♭–G♭–B♭–E♭

Words and Music by Ozzy Osbourne,
Robert Daisley, Zakk Wylde
and Randy Castillo

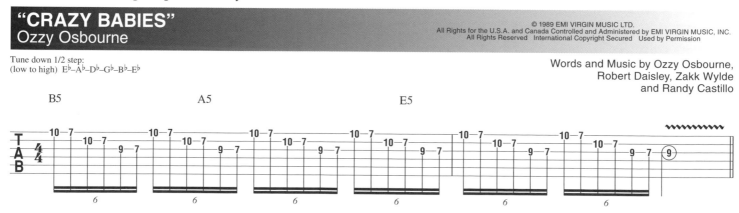

Dorian/Blues Hybrids

The combination of the blues scale and the Dorian mode results in a fingering pattern on the top strings that's often used in rock. Here's the pattern in the key of C.

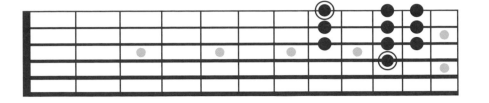

This shape has produced some speedier repeating licks, such as this one, in the vein of Alvin Lee. This lick exploits the tangy 6th degree of the Dorian mode.

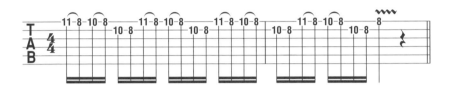

In "Freebird," the boys from Lynyrd Skynyrd do a variation on this lick. Here, the note on the B string is moved up one fret from the 6th to the ♭7th, so the lick isn't quite as tart.

"FREEBIRD"
Lynyrd Skynyrd

Words and Music by Allen Collins
and Ronnie Van Zant

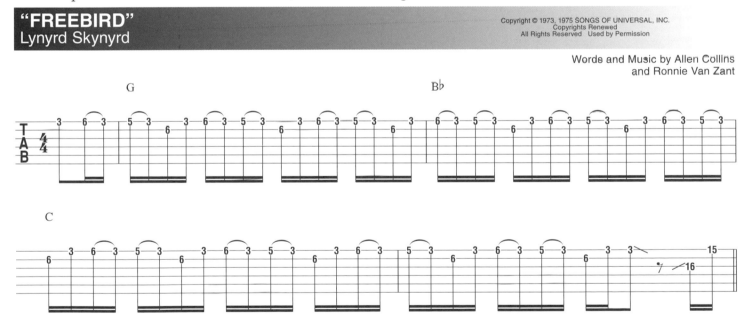

You can play that same type of pattern on each of these top string groups. For example, you could play it on the third and fourth strings to get a blues scale variation.

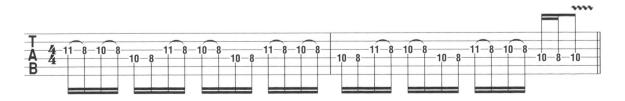

Any similar pattern can be transferred to the middle strings or any adjacent string set. Here's what Lynyrd Skynyrd did in "Sweet Home Alabama."

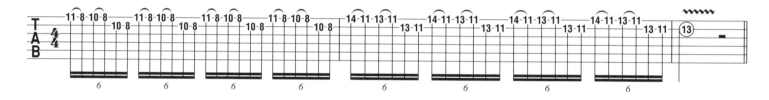

Words and Music by Ronnie Van Zant,
Ed King and Gary Rossington

 When you really want to rip the roof off the joint, you can play this pattern on the top two strings as sextuplets and then move it up a minor 3rd. When you move up, you're actually playing the blues scale pattern we just played, just an octave higher.

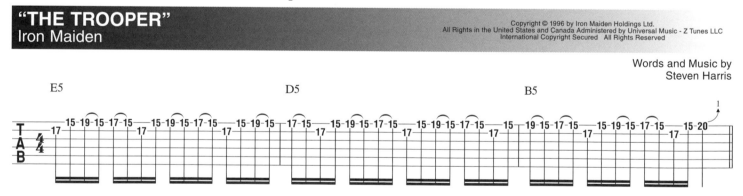

Of course, once you get the hang of this repeating shape, you can create similar variations on your own. Here's what Iron Maiden did on "The Trooper."

Words and Music by
Steven Harris

 Here's a related concept in E. We're playing the same repeating sequence on two different string groups. First will be an E blues sound, then we'll move up to an E Dorian sound. It's just straight alternate picking on this one, so aim for steadiness with your picking.

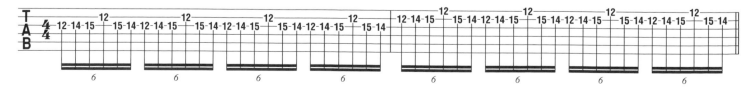

Once you get these ideas down, let them inspire your own similar riffs. You might end up with something like Eddie Van Halen's repeating licks in "Spanish Fly" or "Little Dreamer."

"SPANISH FLY"
Van Halen

Tune down 1 step:
(low to high) D–G–C–F–A–D

Words and Music by David Lee Roth,
Edward Van Halen, Alex Van Halen
and Michael Anthony

"LITTLE DREAMER"
Van Halen

Tune down 1/2 step:
(low to high) E♭–A♭–D♭–G♭–B♭–E♭

Words and Music by David Lee Roth,
Edward Van Halen, Alex Van Halen
and Michael Anthony

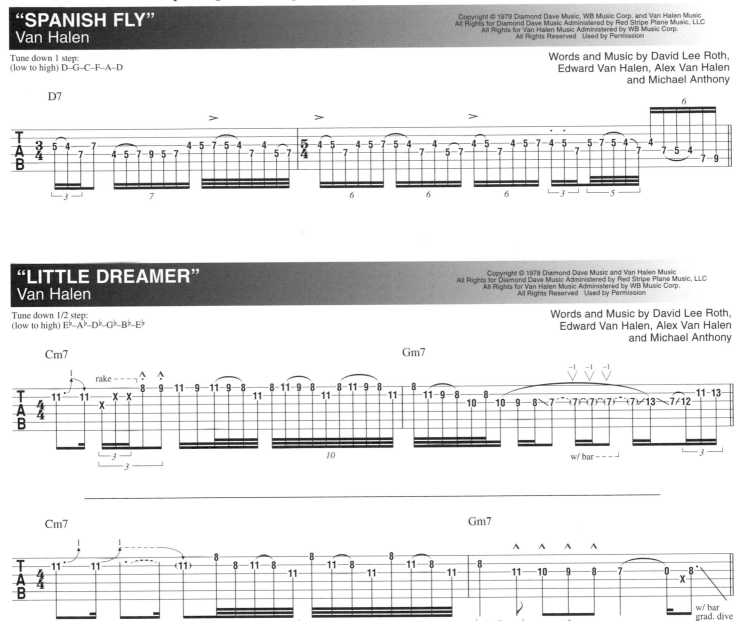

Landing on Your Feet

One very important concept to remember with repeating licks is to "land on your feet." By this we mean that, even if you've nailed the repeating lick beautifully, you'll lose almost all the momentum you've built if you trip up at the end. Then all would have been for naught.

So let's take a look at a few of the licks and how we might come out of them smoothly. In this one, we just used a variation of the lick, which leads to a smooth resolution to the root that we embellish with a slide.

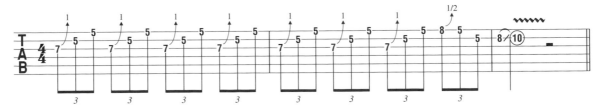

Blues phenom Stevie Ray Vaughan did a similar thing in "Texas Flood," sliding into the unison root on the adjacent lower string.

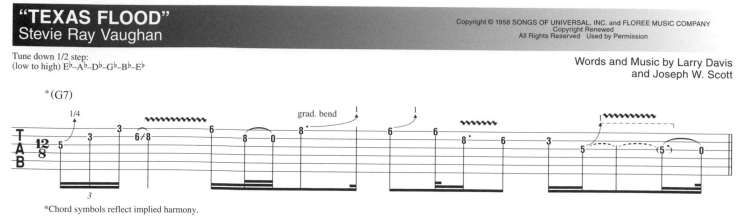

"TEXAS FLOOD"
Stevie Ray Vaughan

Tune down 1/2 step:
(low to high) Eb–Ab–Db–Gb–Bb–Eb

Words and Music by Larry Davis
and Joseph W. Scott

*Chord symbols reflect implied harmony.

 In this next lick, we'll used the effective "reach one higher" device. It's as if you're trying to scale a wall keep just missing the top. Finally, at the end, you stretch and just reach it before coming back down and creating a satisfying conclusion.

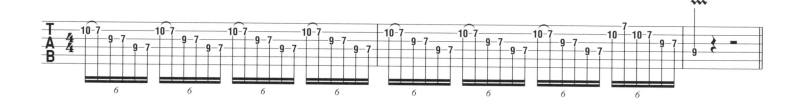

After repeatedly hammering out the high A, which is the b7th, we finally nick the high tonic on the way out before scaling back down to the root.

 And finally, let's take a look at how we might get out of one of our three (or six)-against-four type patterns.

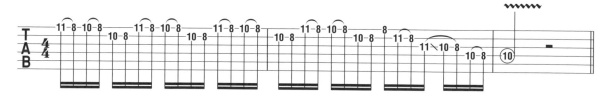

So, on this one, we're releasing the tension in two ways. First, we're settling into a rhythmically clear descent based on straight four-note groupings. Second, we finish off by nailing the root squarely on the downbeat. These two steps solidify both the tonality and the sense of meter.

Of course you could just go from one repeating passage to another as Eddie Van Halen did in "Eruption." You just need to have those kinds of chops, which is easier said than done!

"ERUPTION"
Van Halen

Tune down 1/2 step:
(low to high) E♭–A♭–D♭–G♭–B♭–E♭

Music by David Lee Roth, Edward Van Halen,
Alex Van Halen and Michael Anthony

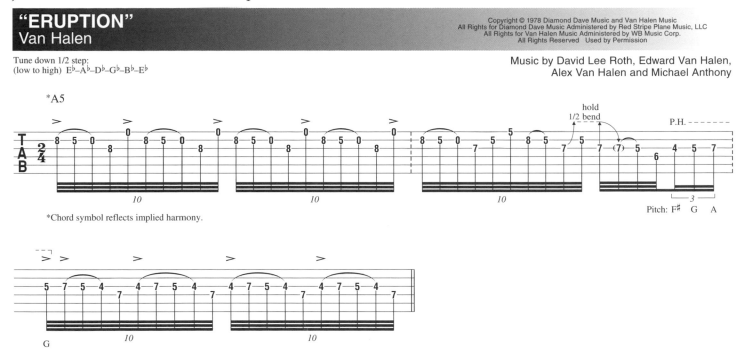

*Chord symbol reflects implied harmony.

Remember that context is what really makes these licks effective. If you just throw them in randomly, they probably won't make much sense. But if you use them to raise the intensity and find a way to smoothly release the tension you've created, you'll create a sense of direction and purpose in your solo.

MIXING SCALES AND MODES

If you've learned all your scales and modes, but are still looking for some ways to get fresh sounds, it's time to mix it up ... literally. In this lesson, we'll learn how you can mix modes to get some great, fresh-sounding licks.

Prime Mixing Conditions

We're going to assume that you're familiar with all the scales we'll cover in this lesson. If not, you can find plenty of fingerings for all of them in resources like scale books or if you search online.

Before we start mixin' it up, let's talk briefly about where it will likely sound best to do so. If you just start haphazardly combining scales, you might not be pleased with the results.

Vamps on One Chord

An extended stay on one harmony is a prime place to try out your modal mixing licks. It helps to keep things from getting too monotonous, and it can create some great tension as well, which is easier said than done with no real chord changes.

For instance, you commonly come across a dominant vamp, like this one in E:

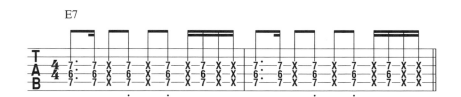

Dominant chords have a major 3rd, but, as evidenced in the blues, our ear will accept the minor 3rd as well. So we can try mixing a major-sounding mode and a minor-sounding mode together to get some interesting sounds.

Here's a lick that combines E Mixolydian with E Dorian. This has a jazzier flavor than just the standard pentatonic approach. It starts off with E Mixolydian in twelfth position and E Dorian for the second half. Since the only difference between the two scales is the 3rd, the difference is pretty subtle. But what a difference! Kinda like putting a dash of salt in your lemonade. Even just a vague hint of the salty flavor will be noticeable. Learn this one and whip it out the next time you jam on some James Brown favorites.

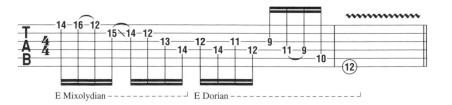

In "She's a Woman," Jeff Beck mixes A Dorian and A Mixolydian.

"SHE'S A WOMAN"
Jeff Beck

Words and Music by John Lennon
and Paul McCartney

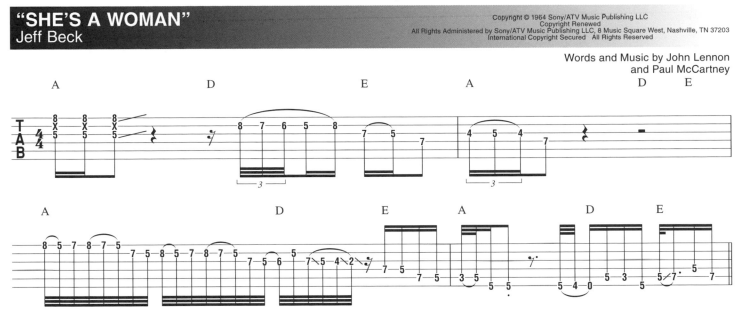

Let's try mixing E Mixolydian with something a little more tart, like E melodic minor. With melodic minor, we've got the major seventh, which is quite an attention grabber over the dominant chord. This combo is not so subtle, and you'll definitely get noticed using it.

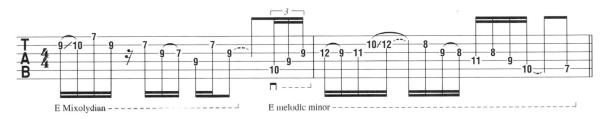

And now let's try starting off with the E blues scale and then moving into E Lydian dominant to shake things up a bit. The Lydian dominant scale really perks your ears up. Notice that, while the ♯4 from the Lydian dominant is used only once, it colors the entire second half of the lick.

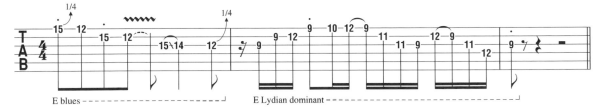

Pedal Tone Vamps

The less specific the harmony is during the vamp, the more wide open the possibilities are. Let's work with a non tonally-specific A pedal groove for the next two examples.

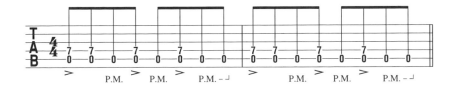

If you work it right, you can get away with just about anything. This is where taste and listening experience will be key factors. Here's an example of A Lydian moving into A whole tone.

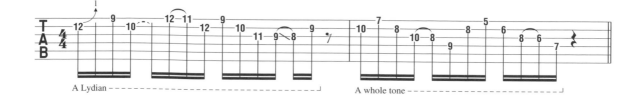

Pretty ear opening, huh? If you really want to wake the audience up, you can take a quick sequence, say, in sextuplets, and repeat it while mixing two different scales. Here, we're playing A Ionian for beats 1 and 2 and then switching to A Lydian dominant on the way back up.

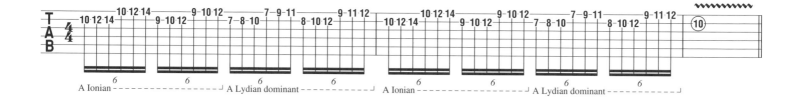

Combining Scales at the Same Time

So far, we've been using one scale for a few beats and then moving to another scale to finish the lick. But what if we think about combining two scales the whole way through? You can get some pretty crazy-sounding things. Let's revisit both our vamps and try that approach.

Over the E7 funk vamp, let's combine E Mixolydian and E melodic minor. Starting with a John Scofield-influenced major 7th leap, we're working our way down from twelfth to seventh position.

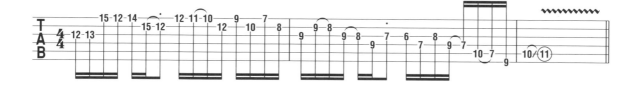

Now let's combine E blues and E Lydian dominant over that vamp. This combo gives you some real ear-grabbing colors.

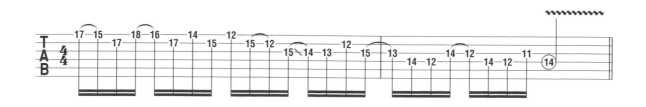

Check out the colors Slash gets in "Sweet Child of Mine" when he mixes A Dorian ♯4 (the fourth mode of harmonic minor) with just regular A Dorian.

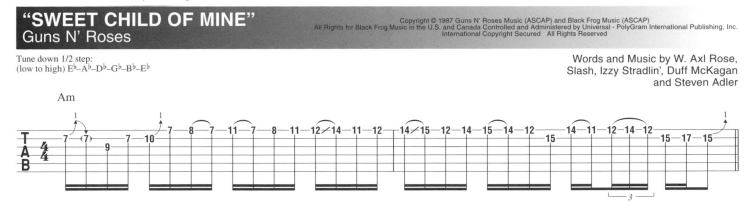

"SWEET CHILD OF MINE"
Guns N' Roses

Tune down 1/2 step:
(low to high) E♭–A♭–D♭–G♭–B♭–E♭

Words and Music by W. Axl Rose,
Slash, Izzy Stradlin', Duff McKagan
and Steven Adler

Let's try a few over our A pedal tone riff. Earlier we looked at A Lydian moving into A whole tone. Here's what it would sound like combining both scales. Can you say "out there?"

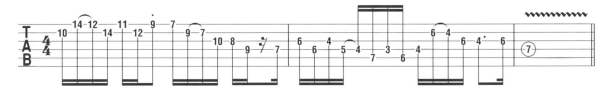

And now let's combine A Phrygian and A Lydian.

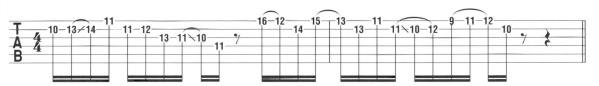

There's lots of craziness going on in there. To the uninitiated, it may sound random and chaotic, but it's all under control. If you look closely at the sum of the combined A Phrygian and Lydian modes, you'll see that we actually have all twelve tones to work with. However, thinking in terms of combining two scales makes it easier to create structured melodies than just thinking of the chromatic scale.

Over an A5 power chord, Steve Hunter mixes up a whole bunch of "A" modes including Lydian, Mixolydian, and Dorian over Aerosmith's "Train Kept A-Rollin'."

"TRAIN KEPT A-ROLLIN'"
Aerosmith

Words and Music by Tiny Bradshaw,
Lois Mann and Howie Kay

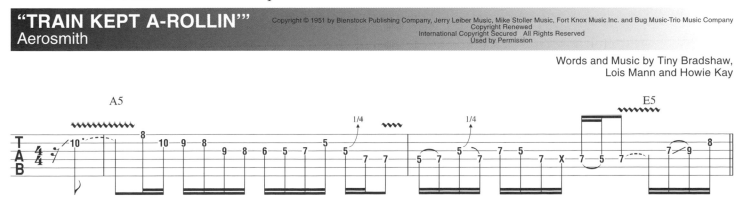

Take some time to experiment with these ideas. You can make this idea as subtle or as crazy outside as you want. Have fun.

PENTATONIC SCALE SUBSTITUTIONS

In this lesson we're going to talk about getting some fresh sounds out of the anything-but-fresh minor pentatonic scale. This is a concept called pentatonic scale substitutions.

Typically, pentatonic scales played on lead guitar are synonymous with rock or blues styles, where one pentatonic scale can be used over all the chord changes. But with pentatonic substitution, you can easily use the familiar pentatonic scale patterns in a variety of soloing applications, most notably jazzier soloing, where we can follow the chord changes. But before we get into that, let's quickly review some basic pentatonic concepts.

Pentatonic Applications

We can apply a major or minor pentatonic scale to any situation where we would normally use a major or natural minor scale. For instance, if we're playing in the key of D major, we can use either a D major scale or a D major pentatonic scale, and they will both sound fine. The D major pentatonic scale has five out of the seven notes of the D major scale (indicated here by the grey numbers).

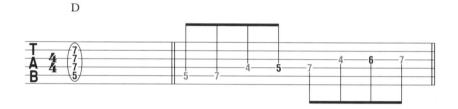

Likewise, if we're playing in C minor, we can use a C minor pentatonic scale or a C natural minor scale. The C minor pentatonic scale has five out of the seven notes of the C natural minor scale.

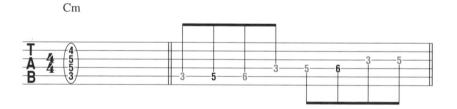

Relative Minor

Also important to know is the idea of the *relative minor*. The relative minor of a major key can be determined by locating the 6th degree of a major scale. So if you're in the key of G major, you can find the relative minor by locating the 6th degree, which is E in this case. Therefore, E minor is the relative minor of G major.

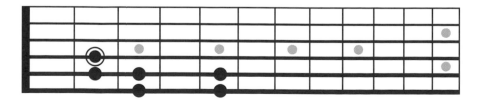

Any major scale and its corresponding relative minor scale contain the exact same notes; they just begin and end on different ones. Likewise, the only difference between a major pentatonic scale and its relative minor pentatonic scale is in the treatment of the notes.

When you're playing D major pentatonic, you're playing the same notes as B minor pentatonic, and vice versa.

Here's D major pentatonic/B minor pentatonic.

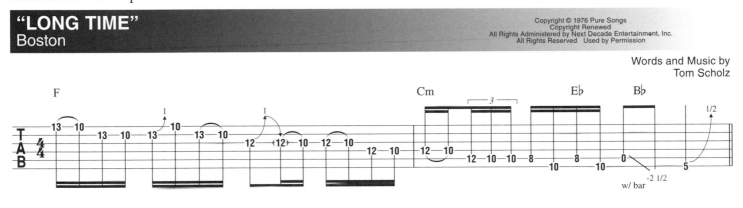

It's the same notes—just different starting points in the pattern.

Check out the relative minor soloing technique in Boston's "Long Time," as Tom Scholz rips off a speedy line from the D minor pentatonic box over the tonic F chord.

"LONG TIME"
Boston

Words and Music by
Tom Scholz

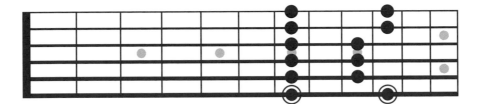

Substitution

That brings us to the concept of substitution. The basic idea here is to use a minor pentatonic scale from a different root over a particular chord to access certain notes that you wouldn't normally find in the standard major or minor pentatonic scale. If we're playing over a C major chord, we've learned so far that we have two choices of scales to play:

The C major scale, and the C major pentatonic scale.

C

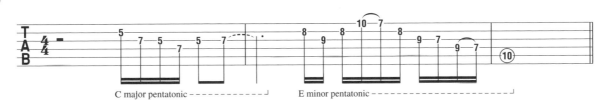

C major pentatonic - - - - - - - - - - ⌐   E minor pentatonic - - - - - - - - - - - - - - - - - - ⌐

Let's say we want to add more color to the solo or melody by applying a Cmaj7 sound over the C major chord. The only difference between the C major triad (C, E, and G) and the Cmaj7 chord tones (C, E, G, and B), is the note B, which is the 7th degree of the C major scale. The C major scale contains the note B, but it also contains notes that we might not want, such as the 4th, F. We *could* just use the C major scale and avoid hitting the tones we don't want, but there is also another method.

23

Substituting off the 3rd of Major Chords

If we were to play a minor pentatonic starting on the 3rd of the C major chord, E, we would end up with E minor pentatonic, which is spelled E–G–A–B–D. The only difference between this scale and the C major pentatonic scale is that the C is now replaced with B, the major 7th. Let's hear how this sounds in an example.

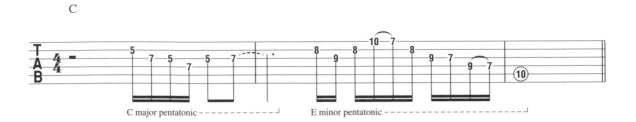

Here's a rock example in the key of C minor where we'll stick with C minor pentatonic until the E♭ major chord, where we'll use a G minor pentatonic scale (G being the 3rd of E♭).

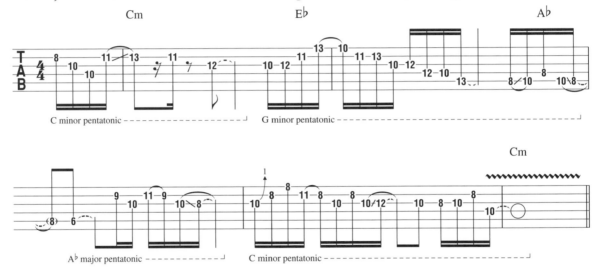

In David Bowie's "Space Oddity," check out how the A minor pentatonic scale is played over the Fmaj7 chord to highlight the major 7th quality.

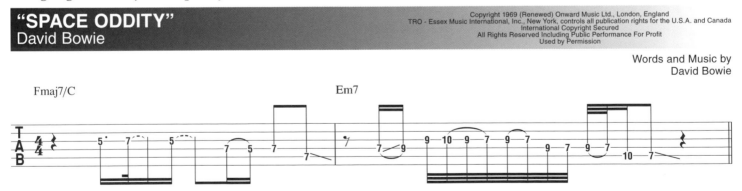

"SPACE ODDITY"
David Bowie

Words and Music by
David Bowie

During the outro solo of Tom Petty's "Runnin' Down a Dream," Mike Campbell rips off a series of quick hammer-on licks from the E minor pentatonic over the C chord, resulting in a bright, Cmaj7 sound.

"RUNNIN' DOWN A DREAM"
Tom Petty

Words and Music by Tom Petty,
Jeff Lynne and Mike Campbell

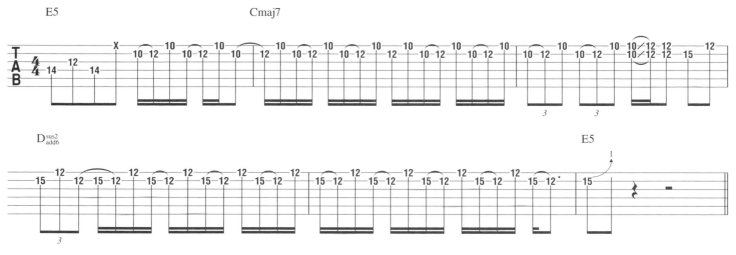

Check out Chicago's Terry Kath as he lays into an A minor pentatonic run over Fmaj7 in "25 or 6 to 4."

"25 OR 6 TO 4"
Chicago

Words and Music by
Robert Lamm

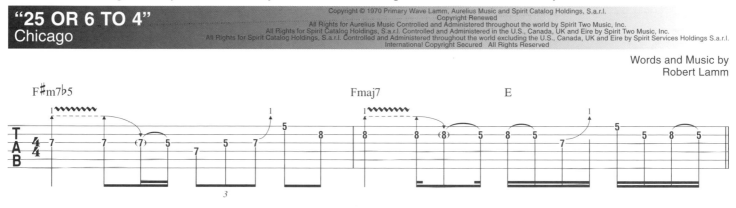

This idea also translates easily to the blues scale. You can use the E blues scale over a Cmaj7 chord as well to give it a bluesy coloring. Here's the E blues scale, which is the same as the minor pentatonic, but with an added ♭5th.

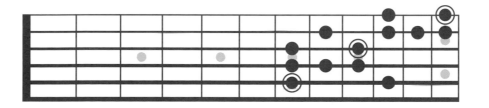

Check It out as a lick over a Cmaj7 harmony.

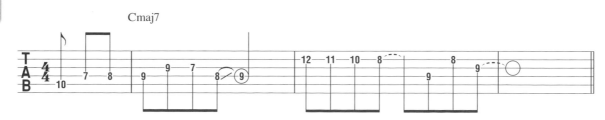

And here's another lick superimposing E blues over Cmaj7. This one's played with a straight, funk-jazz feel. Notice that we go ahead and resolve to the tonic C at the end of the phrase. This is to illustrate that you can pick and choose when you want to use the substitution principle. Just because we started the phrase playing the E blues scale, we don't have to end on it.

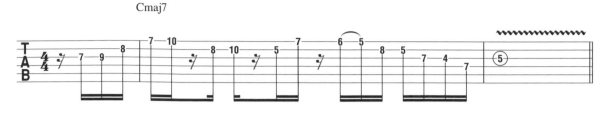

This approach allows you to specifically target the tones you want without having to worry about avoiding other tones in the scale. The idea of scale substitution has basically no limits. Let's check out some of the other substitution methods.

Substituting off the 5th of Minor or Dominant Chords

 If you're soloing over a minor triad, a minor seventh chord, or a dominant chord, you can play the minor pentatonic scale starting on the *5th* of the chord you are playing over. This will accommodate the ♭7th of minor 7th and dominant chords. Check it out in this next jazz-blues example, where we'll play C minor pentatonic over the F7 chord and G minor pentatonic over the C7 chord.

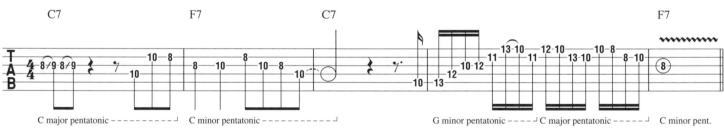

 And here's a funk fusion example where we'll use the same trick over a minor seventh chord. In measure 2, we'll play B minor pentatonic over the Em7 chord, which will give us the note F♯, creating an Em9 sound (E–G–B–D–F♯).

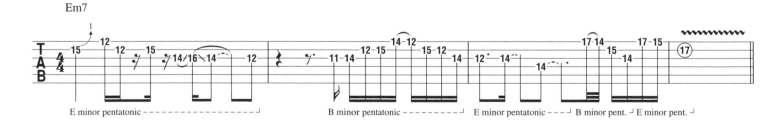

In Styx's "Blue Collar Man," we see this concept illustrated twice in the solo, almost back to back. This first excerpt features the A minor pentatonic over D5 (Dm is implied), creating a Dm9 sound.

"BLUE COLLAR MAN (LONG NIGHTS)"
Styx

Words and Music by
Tommy Shaw

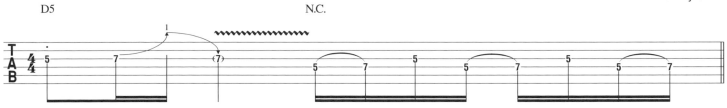

And just a few measures later, the D minor pentatonic scale is used, tastefully incorporating open strings as well, to play over a Gm chord.

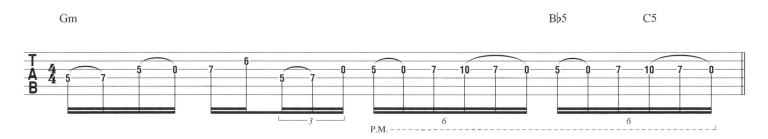

And check out Ritchie Blackmore mining the G minor pentatonic scale over C5 in the immortal classic, "Smoke on the Water.'

"SMOKE ON THE WATER"
Deep Purple

Words and Music by Ritchie Blackmore,
Ian Gillan, Roger Glover, Jon Lord
and Ian Paice

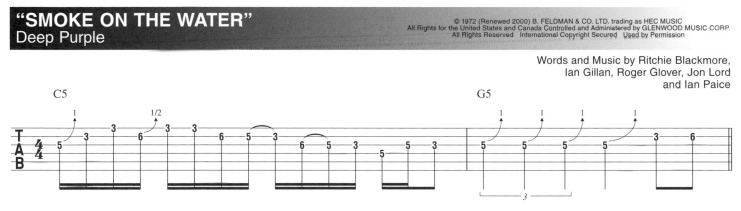

Substituting off the ♯9th of Altered Dominant Chords

The final substitution we'll discuss involves playing minor pentatonic over altered dominant chords. You follow the same process as before but now start with the ♯9th (or ♭3rd) of the chord. For example, if you want to play over an A7♭9♯5 chord:

$$A7^{\flat 9}_{\sharp 5}$$

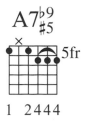

1 2444

The sharp 9th of this chord is C. So you could play a C minor pentatonic scale over this chord and it would highlight almost all altered notes. Check it out:

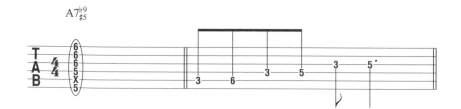

Altered notes for A7 chord derived from the C minor scale:

$$C = {}^{\sharp}9\text{th}$$
$$E^{\flat} = {}^{\flat}5\text{th}$$
$$F = {}^{\sharp}5\text{th}$$
$$G = {}^{\flat}7\text{th}$$
$$B^{\flat} = {}^{\flat}9\text{th}$$

Next we'll play a jazz phrase that uses a pentatonic substitution over each chord of a ii-V-I progression. Over the Em7 chord, we'll use a B minor pentatonic scale to give an Em9 texture. Over A7♭9#5, we'll use the C minor pentatonic to emphasize the altered sound. And over D6, we'll visit the F# blues scale to add the major seventh as well as some other coloring.

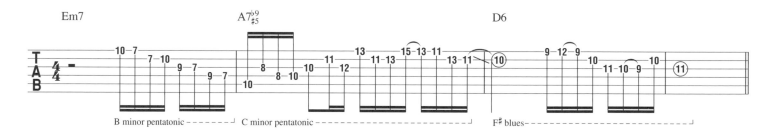

Experimentation is Key

In addition to the concepts we've listed here, feel free to experiment with other substitutions. You could wind up with some fresh, unusual sounds. Let's wrap this lesson up with a couple more examples of how the pros do it. In Godsmack's "Straight Out of Line," we see another concept: using the minor pentatonic (or blues scale) off the major 7th of a major chord. In this case, we have E blues over Fsus2. This results in a colorful Lydian sound.

"STRAIGHT OUT OF LINE"
Godsmack

Drop D tuning, down 1 step:
(low to high) C–G–C–F–A–D

Words and Music by
Sully Erna

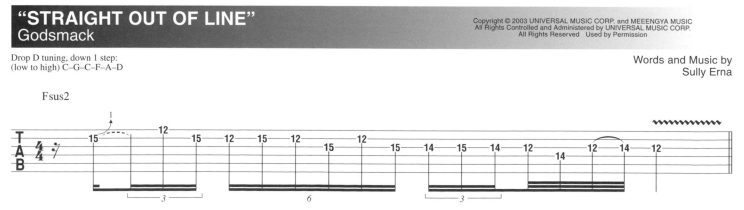

Steve Vai's "The Riddle" is a perfect tune to try out these ideas, as nearly the song takes place over an E pedal. Check out how Vai stretches the ear with this phrase, in which he superimposes F minor pentatonic over E, resulting in a major seven augmented sound.

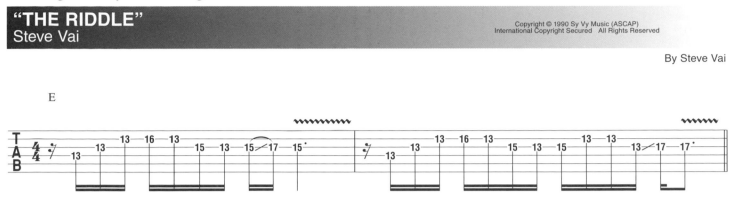

By Steve Vai

Pentatonic Scale substitution is a great way to spice up your solos no matter what style you're playing in. Good luck and have fun with this colorful concept.

RHYTHM TAB LEGEND

Rhythm Tab is a form of notation that adds rhythmic values to the traditional tab staff.

TABLATURE graphically represents the guitar fingerboard. Each horizontal line represents a string, and each number represents a fret. Rhythmic values are shown using ovals, stems, and dots.

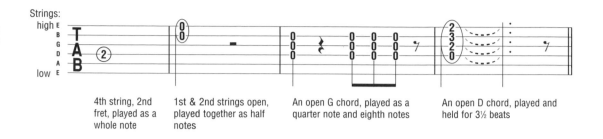

4th string, 2nd fret, played as a whole note

1st & 2nd strings open, played together as half notes

An open G chord, played as a quarter note and eighth notes

An open D chord, played and held for 3½ beats

Definitions for Special Guitar Notation

HALF-STEP BEND: Strike the note and bend up 1/2 step.

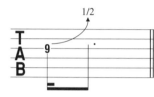

WHOLE-STEP BEND: Strike the note and bend up one step.

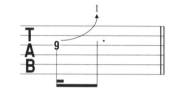

GRACE NOTE BEND: Strike the note and immediately bend up as indicated.

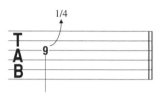

SLIGHT (MICROTONE) BEND: Strike the note and bend up 1/4 step.

BEND AND RELEASE: Strike the note and bend up as indicated, then release back to the original note. Only the first note is struck.

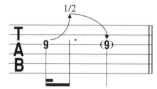

PRE-BEND: Bend the note as indicated, then strike it.

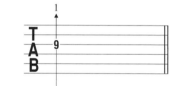

PRE-BEND AND RELEASE: Bend the note as indicated. Strike it and release the bend back to the original note.

UNISON BEND: Strike the two notes simultaneously and bend the lower note up to the pitch of the higher.

HOLD BEND: While sustaining bent note, strike note on different string.

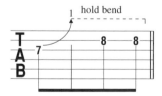

VIBRATO: The string is vibrated by rapidly bending and releasing the note with the fretting hand.

WIDE VIBRATO: The pitch is varied to a greater degree by vibrating with the fretting hand.

HAMMER-ON: Strike the first (lower) note with one finger, then sound the higher note (on the same string) with another finger by fretting it without picking.

PULL-OFF: Place both fingers on the notes to be sounded. Strike the first note and without picking, pull the finger off to sound the second (lower) note.

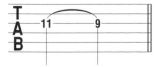

HAMMER FROM NOWHERE: Sound note(s) by hammering with fret hand finger only.

GRACE NOTE SLUR: Strike the note and immediately hammer-on (or pull-off) as indicated.

GRACE NOTE SLUR (CLUSTER): Strike the notes and immediately hammer-on (or pull-off) as indicated.

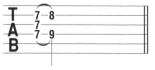

LEGATO SLIDE: Strike the first note and then slide the same fret-hand finger up or down to the second note. The second note is not struck.

SHIFT SLIDE: Same as legato slide, except the second note is struck.

TRILL: Very rapidly alternate between the notes indicated by continuously hammering on and pulling off.

TAPPING: Hammer ("tap") the fret indicated with the pick-hand index or middle finger and pull off to the note fretted by the fret hand.

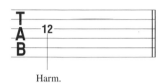

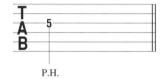

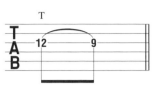

NATURAL HARMONIC: Strike the note while the fret-hand lightly touches the string directly over the fret indicated.

PINCH HARMONIC: The note is fretted normally and a harmonic is produced by adding the edge of the thumb or the tip of the index finger of the pick hand to the normal pick attack.

HARP HARMONIC: The note is fretted normally and a harmonic is produced by gently resting the pick hand's index finger directly above the indicated fret (in parentheses) while the pick hand's thumb or pick assists by plucking the appropriate string.

PICK SCRAPE: The edge of the pick is rubbed down (or up) the string, producing a scratchy sound.

Harm.

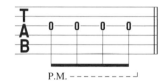

P.H.

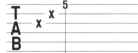

H.H.

P.S.

MUFFLED STRINGS: A percussive sound is produced by laying the fret hand across the string(s) without depressing, and striking them with the pick hand.

PALM MUTING: The note is partially muted by the pick hand lightly touching the string(s) just before the bridge.

RAKE: Drag the pick across the strings indicated with a single motion.

TREMOLO PICKING: The note is picked as rapidly and continuously as possible.

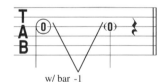

P.M. - - - - - - - -

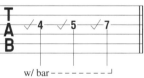

rake - - ⌐

ARPEGGIATE: Play the notes of the chord indicated by quickly rolling them from bottom to top.

VIBRATO BAR DIVE AND RETURN: The pitch of the note or chord is dropped a specified number of steps (in rhythm), then returned to the original pitch.

VIBRATO BAR SCOOP: Depress the bar just before striking the note, then quickly release the bar.

VIBRATO BAR DIP: Strike the note and then immediately drop a specified number of steps, then release back to the original pitch.

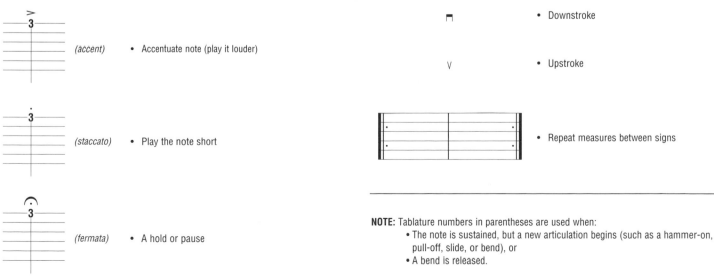

w/ bar -1

w/ bar - - - - - - - ⌐

w/ bar - - - - - - ⌐

Additional Musical Definitions

(accent) • Accentuate note (play it louder)

(staccato) • Play the note short

(fermata) • A hold or pause

⊓ • Downstroke

V • Upstroke

• Repeat measures between signs

NOTE: Tablature numbers in parentheses are used when:
  • The note is sustained, but a new articulation begins (such as a hammer-on, pull-off, slide, or bend), or
  • A bend is released.

HAL•LEONARD GUITAR PLAY-ALONG®

This series will help you play your favorite songs quickly and easily. Just follow the tab and listen to the CD to hear how the guitar should sound, and then play along using the separate backing tracks. Mac or PC users can also slow down the tempo without changing pitch by using the CD in their computer. The melody and lyrics are included in the book so that you can sing or simply follow along.

INCLUDES TAB

VOL. 1 – ROCK 00699570 / $16.99
VOL. 2 – ACOUSTIC 00699569 / $16.95
VOL. 3 – HARD ROCK 00699573 / $16.95
VOL. 4 – POP/ROCK 00699571 / $16.99
VOL. 5 – MODERN ROCK 00699574 / $16.99
VOL. 6 – '90s ROCK 00699572 / $16.99
VOL. 7 – BLUES 00699575 / $16.95
VOL. 8 – ROCK 00699585 / $14.99
VOL. 9 – PUNK ROCK 00699576 / $14.95
VOL. 10 – ACOUSTIC 00699586 / $16.95
VOL. 11 – EARLY ROCK 00699579 / $14.95
VOL. 12 – POP/ROCK 00699587 / $14.95
VOL. 13 – FOLK ROCK 00699581 / $14.95
VOL. 14 – BLUES ROCK 00699582 / $16.95
VOL. 15 – R&B 00699583 / $14.95
VOL. 16 – JAZZ 00699584 / $15.95
VOL. 17 – COUNTRY 00699588 / $15.95
VOL. 18 – ACOUSTIC ROCK 00699577 / $15.95
VOL. 19 – SOUL 00699578 / $14.95
VOL. 20 – ROCKABILLY 00699580 / $14.95
VOL. 21 – YULETIDE 00699602 / $14.95
VOL. 22 – CHRISTMAS 00699600 / $15.95
VOL. 23 – SURF 00699635 / $14.95
VOL. 24 – ERIC CLAPTON 00699649 / $17.99
VOL. 25 – LENNON & McCARTNEY 00699642 / $16.99
VOL. 26 – ELVIS PRESLEY 00699643 / $14.95
VOL. 27 – DAVID LEE ROTH 00699645 / $16.95
VOL. 28 – GREG KOCH 00699646 / $14.95
VOL. 29 – BOB SEGER 00699647 / $14.95
VOL. 30 – KISS 00699644 / $16.99
VOL. 31 – CHRISTMAS HITS 00699652 / $14.95
VOL. 32 – THE OFFSPRING 00699653 / $14.95
VOL. 33 – ACOUSTIC CLASSICS 00699656 / $16.95
VOL. 34 – CLASSIC ROCK 00699658 / $16.95
VOL. 35 – HAIR METAL 00699660 / $16.95
VOL. 36 – SOUTHERN ROCK 00699661 / $16.95
VOL. 37 – ACOUSTIC METAL 00699662 / $16.95
VOL. 38 – BLUES 00699663 / $16.95
VOL. 39 – '80s METAL 00699664 / $16.99
VOL. 40 – INCUBUS 00699668 / $17.95
VOL. 41 – ERIC CLAPTON 00699669 / $16.95
VOL. 42 – 2000s ROCK 00699670 / $16.99
VOL. 43 – LYNYRD SKYNYRD 00699681 / $17.95
VOL. 44 – JAZZ 00699689 / $14.99
VOL. 45 – TV THEMES 00699718 / $14.95
VOL. 46 – MAINSTREAM ROCK 00699722 / $16.95

VOL. 47 – HENDRIX SMASH HITS 00699723 / $19.95
VOL. 48 – AEROSMITH CLASSICS 00699724 / $17.99
VOL. 49 – STEVIE RAY VAUGHAN 00699725 / $17.99
VOL. 50 – 2000s METAL 00699726 / $16.99
VOL. 51 – ALTERNATIVE '90s 00699727 / $12.95
VOL. 52 – FUNK 00699728 / $14.95
VOL. 53 – DISCO 00699729 / $14.99
VOL. 54 – HEAVY METAL 00699730 / $14.95
VOL. 55 – POP METAL 00699731 / $14.95
VOL. 56 – FOO FIGHTERS 00699749 / $14.95
VOL. 57 – SYSTEM OF A DOWN 00699751 / $14.95
VOL. 58 – BLINK-182 00699772 / $14.95
VOL. 60 – 3 DOORS DOWN 00699774 / $14.95
VOL. 61 – SLIPKNOT 00699775 / $14.95
VOL. 62 – CHRISTMAS CAROLS 00699798 / $12.95
VOL. 63 – CREEDENCE CLEARWATER REVIVAL 00699802 / $16.99
VOL. 64 – THE ULTIMATE OZZY OSBOURNE 00699803 / $16.99
VOL. 65 – THE DOORS 00699806 / $16.99
VOL. 66 – THE ROLLING STONES 00699807 / $16.95
VOL. 67 – BLACK SABBATH 00699808 / $16.99
VOL. 68 – PINK FLOYD – DARK SIDE OF THE MOON 00699809 / $16.99
VOL. 69 – ACOUSTIC FAVORITES 00699810 / $14.95
VOL. 70 – OZZY OSBOURNE 00699805 / $16.99
VOL. 71 – CHRISTIAN ROCK 00699824 / $14.95
VOL. 72 – ACOUSTIC '90S 00699827 / $14.95
VOL. 73 – BLUESY ROCK 00699829 / $16.99
VOL. 74 – PAUL BALOCHE 00699831 / $14.95
VOL. 75 – TOM PETTY 00699882 / $16.99
VOL. 76 – COUNTRY HITS 00699884 / $14.95
VOL. 77 – BLUEGRASS 00699910 / $12.99
VOL. 78 – NIRVANA 00700132 / $16.99
VOL. 80 – ACOUSTIC ANTHOLOGY 00700175 / $19.95
VOL. 81 – ROCK ANTHOLOGY 00700176 / $22.99
VOL. 82 – EASY SONGS 00700177 / $12.99
VOL. 83 – THREE CHORD SONGS 00700178 / $16.99
VOL. 84 – STEELY DAN 00700200 / $16.99
VOL. 85 – THE POLICE 00700269 /$16.99
VOL. 86 – BOSTON 00700465 / $16.99
VOL. 87 – ACOUSTIC WOMEN 00700763 / $14.99
VOL. 88 – GRUNGE 00700467 / $16.99

VOL. 91 – BLUES INSTRUMENTALS 00700505 / $14.99
VOL. 92 – EARLY ROCK INSTRUMENTALS 00700506 / $12.99
VOL. 93 – ROCK INSTRUMENTALS 00700507 / $16.99
VOL. 96 – THIRD DAY 00700560 / $14.95
VOL. 97 – ROCK BAND 00700703 / $14.99
VOL. 98 – ROCK BAND 00700704 / $14.95
VOL. 99 – ZZ TOP 00700762 / $16.99
VOL. 100 – B.B. KING 00700466 / $16.99
VOL. 102 – CLASSIC PUNK 00700769 / $14.99
VOL. 103 – SWITCHFOOT 00700773 / $16.99
VOL. 104 – DUANE ALLMAN 00700846 / $16.99
VOL. 106 – WEEZER 00700958 / $14.99
VOL. 107 – CREAM 00701069 / $16.99
VOL. 108 – THE WHO 00701053 / $16.99
VOL. 109 – STEVE MILLER 00701054 / $14.99
VOL. 111 – JOHN MELLENCAMP 00701056 / $14.99
VOL. 113 – JIM CROCE 00701058 / $14.99
VOL. 114 – BON JOVI 00701060 / $14.99
VOL. 115 – JOHNNY CASH 00701070 / $16.99
VOL. 116 – THE VENTURES 00701124 / $14.99
VOL. 119 – AC/DC CLASSICS 00701356 / $17.99
VOL. 120 – PROGRESSIVE ROCK 00701457 / $14.99
VOL. 122 – CROSBY, STILLS & NASH 00701610 / $16.99
VOL. 123 – LENNON & MCCARTNEY ACOUSTIC 00701614 / $16.99
VOL. 124 – MODERN WORSHIP 00701629 / $14.99
VOL. 127 – 1970s ROCK 00701739 / $14.99
VOL. 128 – 1960s ROCK 00701740 / $14.99
VOL. 129 – MEGADETH 00701741 / $14.99
VOL. 130 – IRON MAIDEN 00701742 / $14.99
VOL. 131 – 1990s ROCK 00701743 / $14.99
VOL. 133 – TAYLOR SWIFT 00701894 / $16.99

Complete song lists available online.

Prices, contents, and availability subject to change without notice.

FOR MORE INFORMATION, SEE YOUR LOCAL MUSIC DEALER,
OR WRITE TO:

HAL•LEONARD® CORPORATION
7777 W. BLUEMOUND RD. P.O. BOX 13819 MILWAUKEE, WI 53213

Visit Hal Leonard online at www.halleonard.com

0311